Audition Songs for Female Singers 1

D0320279

Wise Publications
London/New York/Paris/Sydney/Copenhagen/Madrid

Exclusive Distributors:
Music Sales Limited
8-9 Frith Street,
London W1V 5TZ, England.
Music Sales Pty Limited
120 Rothschild Avenue,
Rosebery, NSW 2018,
Australia.

Order No. AM92587
ISBN 0-7119-4664-7
This book © Copyright 1997 by Wise Publications

Compiled by Paul Honey and Jack Long
New arrangements by Jack Long
Music processed by Enigma Music Production Services

CD performed and recorded by Paul Honey

Book design by Studio Twenty, London

Printed in the United Kingdom by
Caligraving Limited, Thetford, Norfolk.

Your Guarantee of Quality
As publishers, we strive to produce every book
to the highest commercial standards.
The music has been freshly engraved and the book has been
carefully designed to minimise awkward page turns and
to make playing from it a real pleasure.
Particular care has been given to specifying acid-free,
neutral-sized paper made from pulps which have not been
elemental chlorine bleached. This pulp is from farmed sustainable
forests and was produced with special regard for the environment.
Throughout, the printing and binding have been planned to ensure a
sturdy, attractive publication which should give years of enjoyment.
If your copy fails to meet our high standards, please inform us and
we will gladly replace it.

Music Sales' complete catalogue describes thousands of
titles and is available in full colour sections by subject, direct
from Music Sales Limited. Please state your areas of interest and
send a cheque/postal order for £1.50 for postage to:
Music Sales Limited, Newmarket Road, Bury St. Edmunds,
Suffolk IP33 3YB.

Adelaide's Lament

Words & Music by Frank Loesser

Freely, colla voce

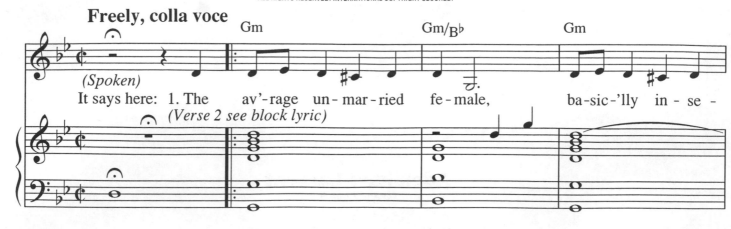

(Spoken)
It says here: 1. The av'rage un-mar-ried fe-male, ba-sic-'lly in-se-
(Verse 2 see block lyric)

-cure Due to some long frus-tra-tion, may re-act With

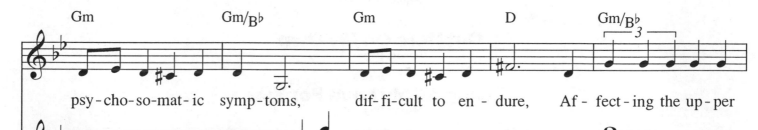

psy-cho-so-mat-ic symp-toms, dif-fi-cult to en-dure, Af-fect-ing the up-per

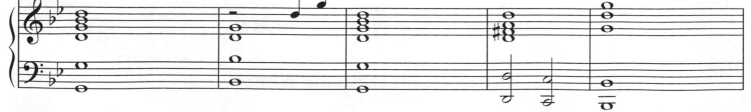

res-pi-ra-to-ry tract. In

oth - er words,__ just from wait-ing a-round for that plain lit - tle band of gold, A

(Verse 3 see block lyric)

per - son___ can de - vel - op a cold. You can

spray her wher - ev - er you fig - ure the strep - to - coc - ci lurk;__ You can

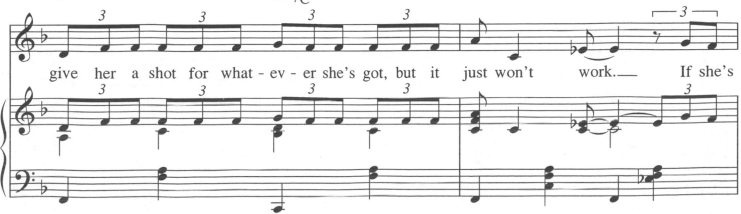

give her a shot for what - ev - er she's got, but it just won't work.__ If she's

5

feel-ing she's get-ting too old, A per-son___ can de-vel-op a bad bad

cold.___

Verse 2
The female remaining single, just in the legal sense,
Shows a neurotic tendency. See note. (Spoken) Note.
Chronic organic syndromes, toxic or hypertense,
Involving the eye, the ear, and the nose and the throat.
In other words, just from worrying whether the wedding is on or off,
A person can develop a cough!
You can feed her all day with the Vitamin A and the Bromo Fizz,
But the medicine never gets anywhere near where the trouble is.
If she's getting a kind of a name for herself, and the name ain't his,
A person can develop a cough!

Verse 3
And furthermore, just from stalling and stalling and stalling the wedding trip,
A person can develop La grippe!
When they get on the train for Niag'ra and she can hear church bells chime,
The compartment is air-conditioned and the mood sublime,
Then they get off at Saratoga for the fourteenth time,
A person can develop La grippe,
La grippe, La post-nasal drip, etc.

Don't Cry For Me Argentina

Music by Andrew Lloyd Webber
Lyrics by Tim Rice

Slowly (♩ = 78)

1. It won't be

ea-sy, you'll think it strange When I try to ex-plain how I feel, That I

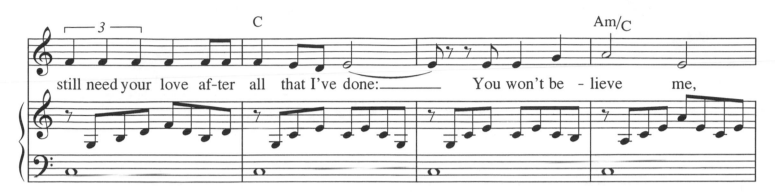

still need your love af-ter all that I've done:_____ You won't be - lieve me,

All you will see is a girl you once knew, Al - though she's dressed up to the

nines at six-es and se-vens with you. 2. I had to let it

hap-pen, I had to change; Could-n't stay all my life down at heel: Look-ing

out of the win-dow, stay - ing out of the sun. So I chose free - dom,

Run-ning a round try-ing ev-ry-thing new; but no - thing im-pressed me at all, I

Slow Tango feel

nev - er ex - pect-ed it to. Don't cry for me Ar-gen - ti - na,____ the

truth is I nev - er left you: All through my wild days, my mad ex -

-ist-ence, I kept my prom-ise, Don't keep your dis-tance.

3. And as for for-tune and as for fame — I nev-er in-vi-ted them in: Though it seemed to the world they were all I de-sired. They are il--lu - - sions,_ they're not the so-lu - tions they prom-ised to be, the

poco rall.

an-swer was here all the time_____ I love you and hope you love me. *ten.*

Slower

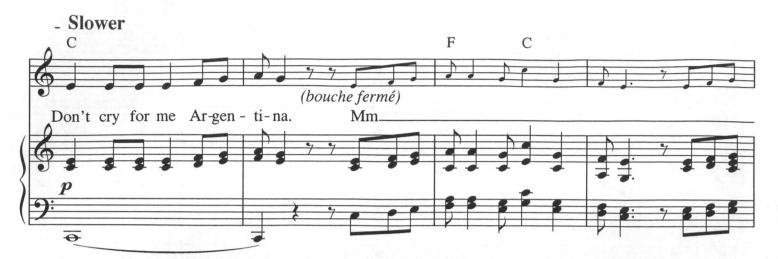

Don't cry for me Ar-gen - ti-na. (bouche fermé) Mm

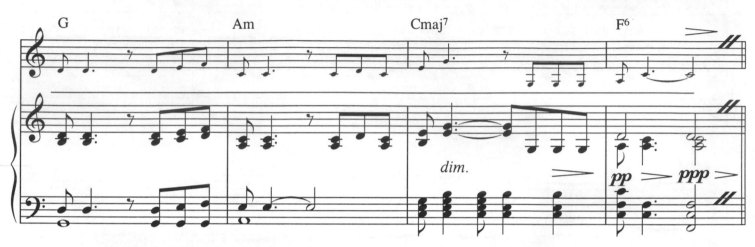

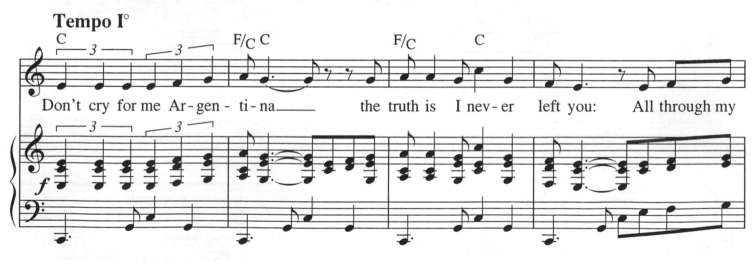

Tempo I°

Don't cry for me Ar-gen - ti-na ___ the truth is I nev-er left you: All through my

wild days   my mad ex - ist-ence,   I kept my prom-ise,   Don't keep your dis - tance. __

Have I said too much? There's no-thing more I can think of to say to you

But all you have to do is

look at me to know that ev-'ry word is true.

Heaven Help My Heart

Words & Music by Benny Andersson, Tim Rice & Bjorn Ulvaeus

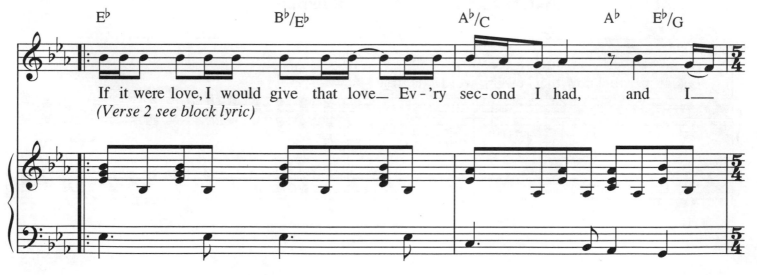

If it were love, I would give that love Ev-'ry sec-ond I had, and I
(Verse 2 see block lyric)

do. Did I know where he'd lead me to? Did I

plan Do-ing all of this for the love of a man?__ Well, I let it

hap-pen an-y-how;__ And what I'm feel-ing now Has no eas-y ex-pla-na-tion,

Rea-son plays__ no__ part. Hea-ven help my__ heart!_____ I

love him too much. What if he saw__ my whole ex-ist-ence

Turn -ing a- round___ a word, a smile, a touch?_____

mind.　　　　　　May-be it's best___ to love___ a stran-ger;_____ But

that's what I've done, Hea -ven help my___ heart!

Molto rit.

Hea - ven help my heart.

Verse 2

One of these days, and it won't be long,
He'll know more about me than he should.
All my dreams will be understood:
No surprise.
Nothing more to learn from the look in my eyes.
Don't you know that time is not my friend?
I'll fight it to the end,
Hoping to keep the best of moments
When the passions start.
Heaven help my heart
The day that I find
Suddenly I've run out of secrets,
Suddenly I'm not always on his mind!

Big Spender

Words by Dorothy Fields
Music by Cy Coleman

The min-ute you walked in the joint, I could see you were a man of dis-tinc-tion,— a real big spend - er;__ Good look ing,_ so re - fined._ Say, would-n't you like to know what's go-ing on in my mind?_ So let me get right to the point.

I don't pop my cork for ev'-ry guy I see.___

To ⊕ *Coda*

Hey! Big Spen-der,___ Spend a lit-tle time___ with

me. Would-n't you like to have

fun, fun, fun? How's a-bout a few laughs, laughs? I can show you a

good time,_____ Let me show you a_____ good time._____ The min-ute you

D. %. al Coda

⊕ CODA

(N.C.)

Hey, Big Spen-der_____ Hey, Big Spen-der!_____

Spend_____ a lit-tle time__ with me, Spend a lit-tle time__ with

me, Spend a lit-tle time__ with me._____

I Will Survive

Words & Music by Dino Fekaris & Freddie Perren

At first I was a-fraid, I was pet-ri-fied,___ kept think-in'
I could nev-er live___ with-out you by my side; but then I spent so ma-ny nights___ think-in'
how you did me wrong, and I grew strong and I learned how to get a-long.___ And so you're

back from out-er space_ I just walked in to find_ you here with that_ sad
me, some bod-y new,_ I'm not that chained up lit-tle per - son_ still in love_

look up-on_your face. I should have changed_ that stu - pid lock,_ I should have made_
_ with you;_ and so you feel like drop -pin' in_ and just ex -

_ you leave your key_ if I'd -'ve known_ for just_ one sec - ond you'd be
-pect me to be free,_ now I'm sav - in' all_ my lov - in' for some

back to both - er me._ Go on now } Go walk out the door_ just turn a-round_
one who's lov-in' me._ Go on now }

now 'cause you're not wel-come an-y-more._ Weren't you the one_ who tried to hurt_

_ me with good - bye? Did I crum - ble,_ did you think I'd lay down_ and die? Oh no, not

I. I will sur - vive,__ oh_ as long as I know how to love_ I

know I'll stay a-live. I've got all my life to live, I've got all my love to give_ and I'll sur- vive._

To ◆ Coda

I will sur-vive.____ Hey, hey!____

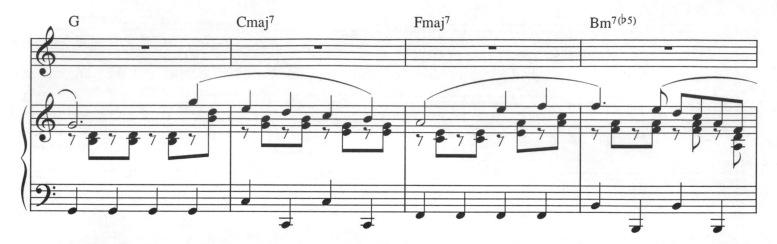

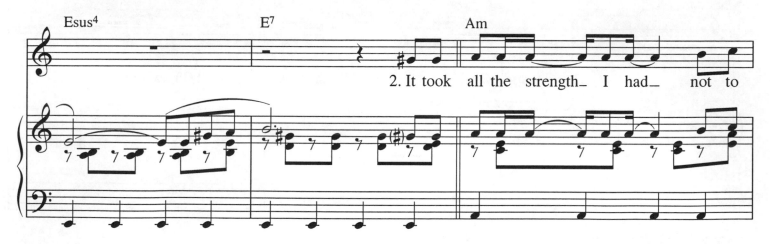

2. It took all the strength__ I had__ not to

fall a-part,_____ kept try-in' hard to mend__ the piec-es of my bro-

Cmaj⁷ ... Fmaj⁷

- ken heart;— and I spent oh so man-y nights— just feel-in'

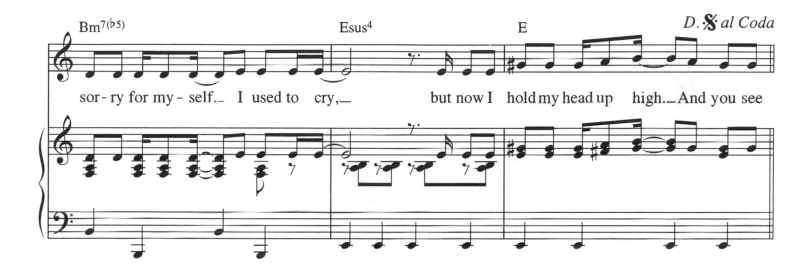

Bm⁷⁽♭⁵⁾ ... Esus⁴ ... E ... *D. 𝄋 al Coda*

sor-ry for my-self.— I used to cry,— but now I hold my head up high.—And you see

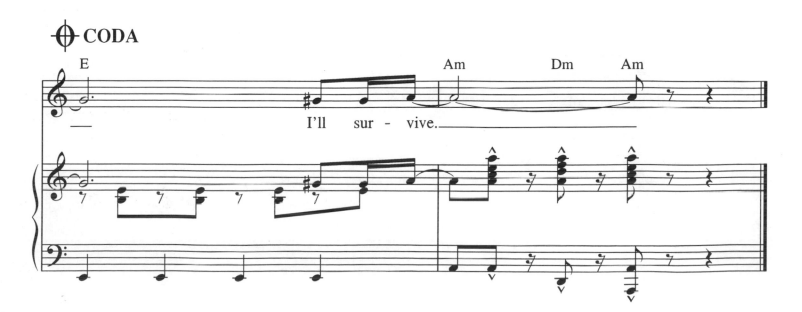

CODA

E ... Am ... Dm ... Am

— I'll sur-vive._____

I Cain't Say No

Words by Oscar Hammerstein II
Music by Richard Rodgers

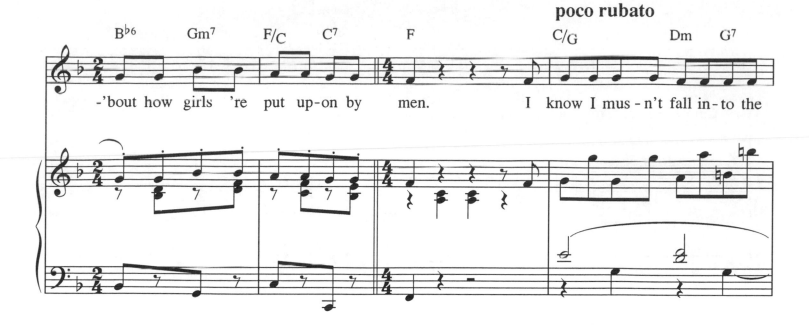

poco rubato

-'bout how girls 're put up-on by men. I know I mus-n't fall in-to the

a tempo (♩ = 128)

pit,_____ But when I'm with a fel-ler I fer - git!

I'm jist a girl who cain't say no,
I'm jist a girl who cain't say no,

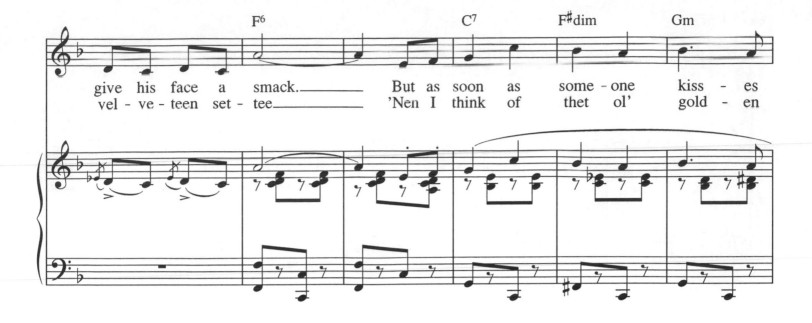

give his face a smack._____ But as soon as some - one kiss - es
vel - ve - teen set - tee_____ 'Nen I think of thet ol' gold - en

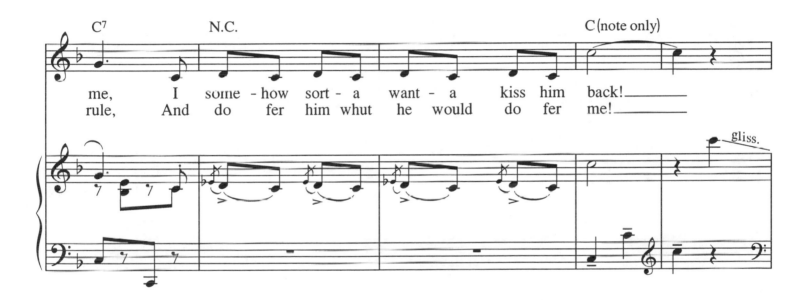

me, I some - how sort - a want - a kiss him back!_____
rule, And do fer him whut he would do fer me!_____

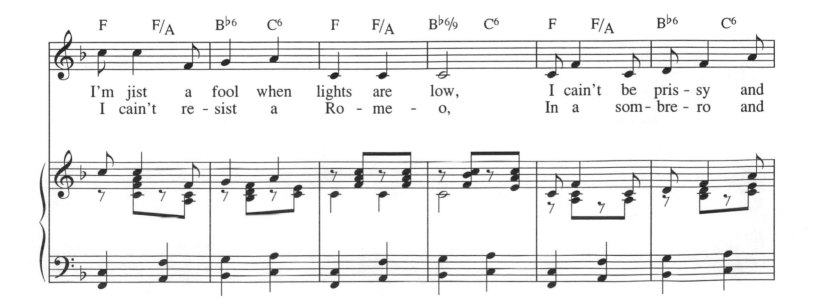

I'm jist a fool when lights are low, I cain't be pris - sy and
I cain't re - sist a Ro - me - o, In a som - bre - ro and

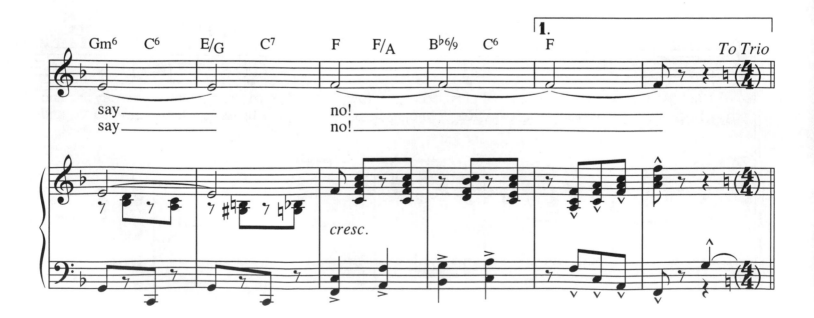

S'pos-in' 'at he says 'at yer sweet-er 'n cream and he's got-ta have cream or

die? Whut you goin' to do when he talks thet way?

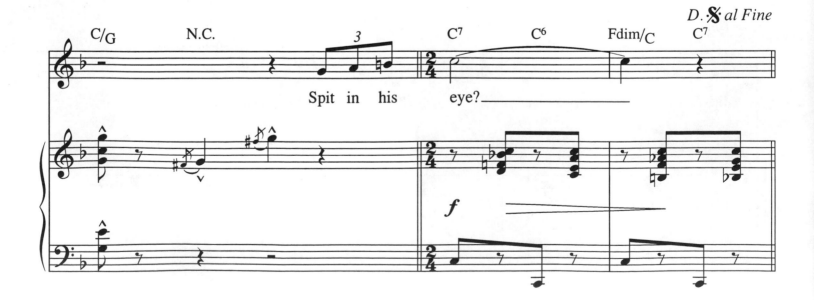

Spit in his eye?_____

D. %: al Fine

Out Here On My Own

Words & Music by Michael Gore & Lesley Gore

Some-times I won-der where I've been, who I am,

do I fit in. Make be-lieve-in' is hard a-lone, out here on my

own. We're al-ways prov-in' who we are,
Un-til the morn-ing sun ap-pears,

Help me through.__ Help me need you.   me need you.

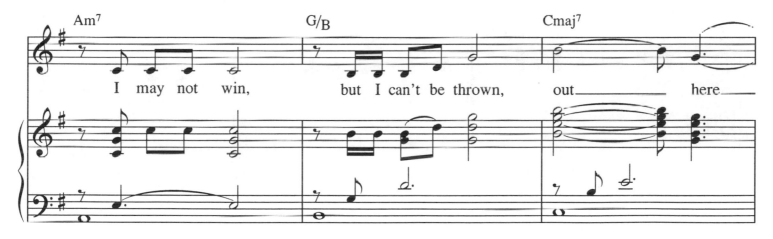

Some-times I won-der   where I've been,   who I am,   do I fit in.

I may not win,   but I can't be thrown,   out_____ here_____

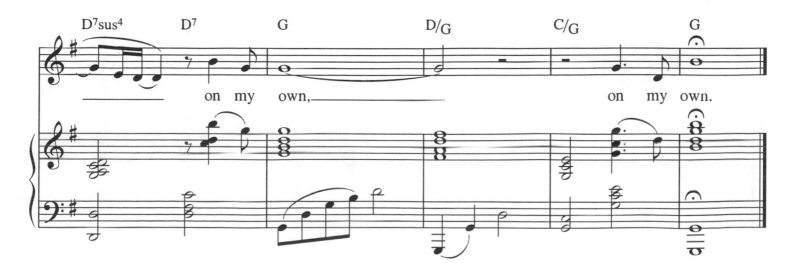

_____ on my own,_____   on my own.

Saving All My Love For You

Words & Music by Gerry Goffin & Michael Masser

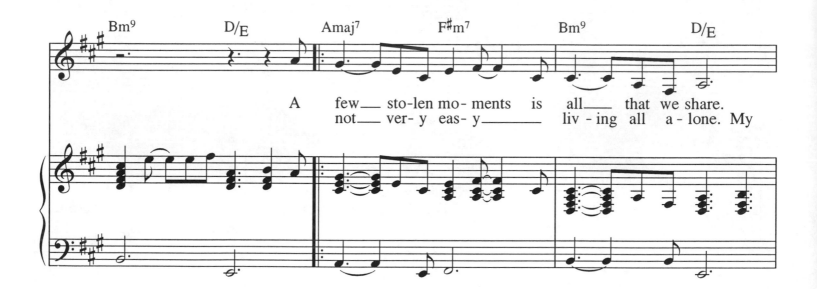

A few stolen moments is all that we share.
not very easy living all alone. My

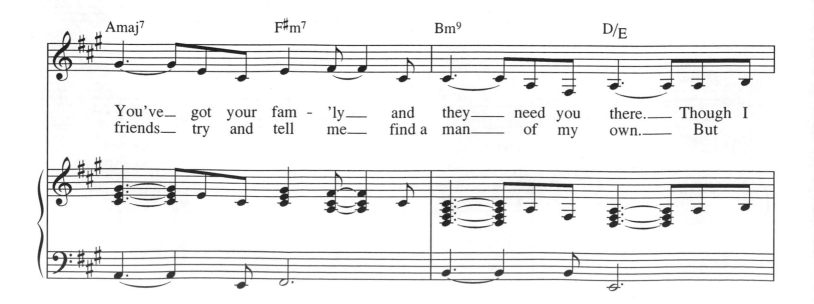

You've got your family and they need you there. Though I
friends try and tell me find a man of my own. But

try___ to re - sist,___ be - ing last___ on your list, but
each___ time I try,___ I just break___ down and cry, 'cause I'd

no oth - er man's___ gon - na do.___ So I'm
rath - er be home___ feel - in' blue.___

sav - ing all my love for you.___

few—— min - utes more.—— Gon - na get—— that old feel - ing—— when you

walk—— through that door.—— 'Cause to - night—— is the night—— for——

feel - - ing all right.—— We'll be mak - ing love the whole night——

through,——————— so I'm sav - ing all my love, yes I'm sav - ing all my love, yes I'm

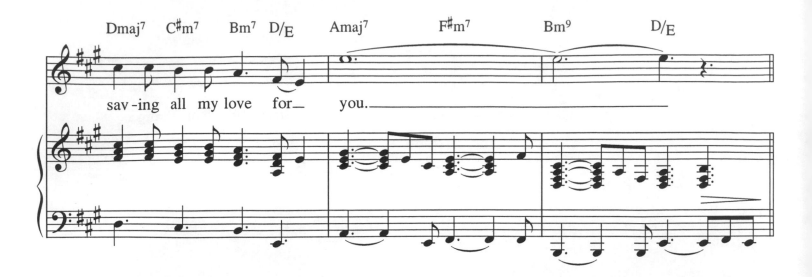

Dmaj7 C#m7 Bm7 D/E Amaj7 F#m7 Bm9 D/E

sav -ing all my love for— you.

Amaj7 F#m7 Bm9 D/E

No oth - er wo - man— is gon - na love you more.— 'Cause to -

F#m7 B/F# F#m7 B/F#

night— is the night— that I'm feel - - ing all right.— We'll be

A F#m7 G#m7 C#9(b5) C#9

mak - ing love the whole— night— through;— so I'm

sav - ing all my love, yes I'm sav - ing all my lov - ing, — yes I'm

sav - ing all my love for you. _____ For

rall.

you. _____

Someone To Watch Over Me

Music & Lyrics by George Gershwin & Ira Gershwin

1. There's a some-bo-dy I'm long-ing to see: I hope that he turns out to be
2. I'm a lit-tle lamb who's lost in the wood; I know I could al-ways be good

Some-one who'll watch ov-er me.
To one who'll watch ov-er me.

Al-though he may not be the man some girls think of as

The Wind Beneath My Wings

Words & Music by Jeff Silbar & Larry Henley

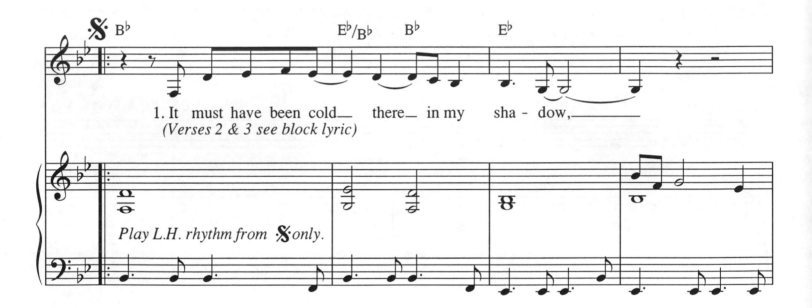

1. It must have been cold— there— in my sha - dow,———
(Verses 2 & 3 see block lyric)

Play L.H. rhythm from 𝄋 only.

To nev - er have sun - light— on your face.———

You were con-tent__ to let me shine.__

You al-ways walked__ a step be-hind.__

to hide the pain.__ Did you ev-er know__

__ that you're my he-ro, And ev-'ry-thing I__

would like to be?_____ I can fly high-

- - - er than an ea - gle,_____ If you are the wind_

To Coda

D.S. (as 2nd time) al Coda

be-neath my wings._____

CODA

wings._____ Did I ev - er tell___ you you're my__

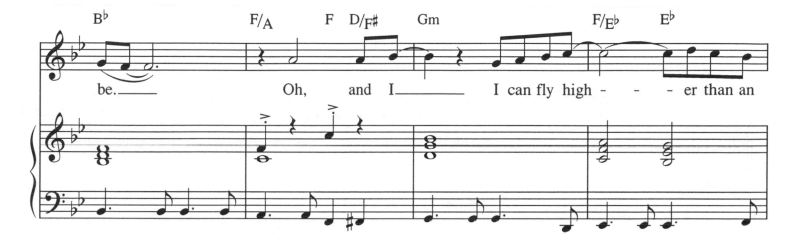

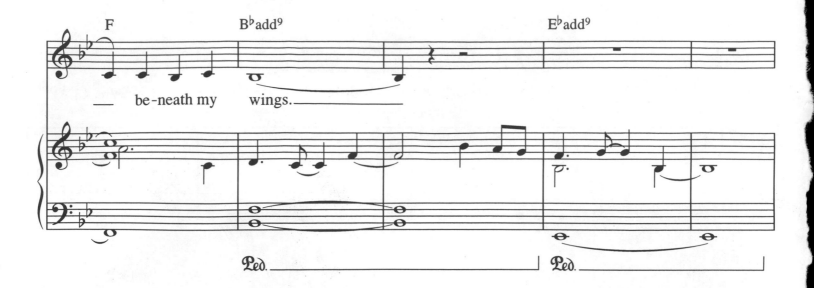

be-neath my wings.

Thank God for you,_ the wind be-neath_ my wings.

Verse 2

So I was the one with all the glory,
While you were the one with all the strain;
A beautiful face without a name,
A beautiful smile to hide the pain.
Did you ever know, etc.

Verse 3

It might have appeared to go unnoticed,
But I've got it all here in my heart.
I want you to know I know the truth:
I would be nothing without you.
Did you ever know, etc.

3/02 (43160)